A Noteworthy Americans
Young Readers Biography Book

Lucky Ears

The True Story of Ben Kuroki,
World War II Hero

by Jean A. Lukesh

Field Mouse
PRODUCTIONS
Grand Island/Palmer, NE

No part of this publication may be reproduced, or stored in a retrieval system, or transmitted in any form or by any means, electronic, mechanical, photocopying, recording, or otherwise, without the permission in writing from the publisher/author.

Copyright © 2010 Jean A. Lukesh
Cover ©2010 by Ronald E. Lukesh

Published by Field Mouse Productions
Grand Island and Palmer, Nebraska
All rights reserved
First Printed, 2010
Printed in the United States of America
Photos: Courtesy of Ben Kuroki, Scott Stewart,
and Bill Kubota, unless otherwise noted. Maps by Ron Lukesh.
This Noteworthy Americans Young Readers biography was designed
by Jean A. Lukesh (Ed.D., Curriculum & Instruction)
and authorized and proofed by Ben Kuroki.
R.L.: 5.5   I.L.: 5 through adult

Cataloging-in-Publication Data
Lukesh, Jean A., 1950—
Lucky Ears: The True Story of Ben Kuroki, World War II Hero
SUMMARY: A young reader's biography of Ben Kuroki, a Nebraska-born, Japanese American who fought very hard to become an American aerial gunner and a hero during World War II. In that war, he flew a total of 58 missions against both Germany and Japan. Throughout his adult life, he often spoke out for good citizenship and against racism. p. cm.
Includes index and select bibliographical references.
Noteworthy Americans Young Readers Biography Series
1. Ben Kuroki, 1917- —Biography—Juvenile. 2. Nebraska—History. 3. Japanese Americans—Biography. 4. Japanese Americans—Nebraska—Biography. 5. World War, 1939-1945—Germany. 6. World War, 1939-1945—Japanese Americans. 7. Nisei. 8. Racial tolerance. 9. Japanese American Soldiers—History—20th Century. 10. United States—Armed Forces—Japanese Americans. 11. United States—Armed Forces—Aerial Gunners.
I. Title.   II. Subtitle.   III. Series.   [A Jean Lukesh Imprint].
D769.8 940.5404 [B][920.71]   ISBN 978-0-9647586-2-9 0-9647586-2-8

This book is dedicated:

To Ben, for "fighting for the right to fight"
for his country, America;

To all the children of Nebraska,
America, and the World;

And to all the men and women
who fight to keep our country free.

Ben Kuroki's Timeline

Year/Day	Ben Kuroki's Timeline	World Timeline
1906	"Sam" Kuroki and Naka Yokoyama come to America from Japan	Major earthquake in San Francisco, California
1907	Sam and Naka meet and marry in Wyoming	
1908	Sam, Naka, and their first child (George) move to Nebraska	
1914		World War I starts
1917, May 16	Ben Kuroki is born	
1918	Kuroki family moves to Hershey, Nebraska farm	World War I ends
1929		Stock Market Crashes, Great Depression begins
1930s		Drought, "Dirty 30s," and Great Depression
1936	Ben graduates from high school	
1937		Japan attacks China
1939		Adolf Hitler (Germany) invades countries in Europe
1941, Dec. 7		Japan attacks Pearl Harbor; World War II starts
1941, Dec.	Ben and Fred join the American Army	Germany declares War on the United States of America
1942	Ben flies in B-24s against Germany	
1944	Ben visits three Internment camps; then flies in B-29s against Japan	
1945, May 8		World War II ends with Germany
1945, Aug.	Ben is injured after the war ends and misses his flight home	World War II ends with Japan
2002	Former Air Corps friends decide to tell the world about Ben	
2006-2008	Ben meets President George W. Bush four times in the White House and is honored by the Smithsonian	
2007	Ben is honored at a PBS Most Honorable Son dinner and video premiere	
2010	Ben is invited to an American Veterans Center Conference in Washington DC	

Table of Contents

Ben Kuroki, an American hero of World War II

Chapter 1:

Introduction to Ben's Lucky Ears

Long ago, Sam Kuroki told his sixth child a secret. He said, "Ben, my son, you have lucky ears."

Sam knew very little English. Ben spoke very little Japanese, but Ben knew what his father meant.

Ben had a tiny hole near the top of each ear. The holes were there when he was born. He was the only one in his family with ears like that.

His family had a **legend** about such ears. The legend said that any boy born in the family with ears like that would be very lucky. The legend said Ben was very special. He would live a long life. And he would be famous. That legend would come true.

Ben was born on a farm in western Nebraska. As a boy, he did not think much of the legend. But as he grew up, many lucky things happened to him. When they did, he often pointed to his lucky ears and laughed.

When Ben was a boy, he thought he might grow up to be a farmer, a truck driver, or a newspaperman. He never dreamed he would become famous as an American war hero and a speaker against **racism**. But he did.

This is the amazing story of Ben Kuroki—a true American war hero, a good **citizen**, and a very lucky man.

Chapter 2:

Born in Nebraska

Ben Kuroki looked Japanese, but he was born in Nebraska. He always thought of himself as an American—just like all his friends and neighbors.

Ben's father came to the United States from Japan in 1906. He came to make a better life for himself.

His first name was Shosuke. Most people could not say that name. They just called Ben's father "Sam" instead.

Sam worked at whatever jobs he could find. Sometimes, he set up pins in a bowling alley.

Sometimes he worked as a janitor. Often he worked for the railroad.

Sam's job took him to Wyoming. There, he met and married Naka Yokoyama in 1907. Naka had also come from Japan in 1906.

Sam and Naka ran a hotel and cafe for railroad workers for a while. They worked hard. They dreamed of having their own farm.

Sam's job then took him to Colorado and Nebraska. He liked the farmland along the Platte River Valley. He and Naka rented a farmhouse and land there in Nebraska.

Their farm was in between the small towns of Gothenburg and Cozad. Ben and most of his older brothers and sisters were born there, on that farm.

All his life, Ben believed he was very lucky to be born in Nebraska and in America. He often said, "I have to thank my Nebraska upbringing and my Nebraska roots for giving me a solid foundation for **patriotism**."

Chapter 3:

Baby Ben and His Family

Ben was the sixth of ten children. He was born on May 16, 1917. But his family did not seem very lucky that day!

Ben was born on the farm. His mother Naka was very sick at that time. Later, a doctor stopped by to see how she and her new baby were doing.

Naka was so sick she could not take care of herself, or her new baby, or her other children. The doctor sent her to a hospital. He left baby Ben at home with the rest of the family.

The doctor saw that the family really needed

help. He sent for a young neighbor woman named Maggie Geiken.

For many weeks after that, Maggie rode her horse to the Kuroki farm three or four times a day to help. She took good care of baby Ben and the other five children. She cooked and cleaned and helped them in many ways.

As a baby, Ben hardly ever cried. When he did, Maggie or Ben's older sister Fuji took care of him. But Fuji was just a young girl, too. She could not help all the time. Sometimes baby Ben just had to suck his thumb for comfort.

When Ben's mother came home from the hospital, she was still very weak. She was not strong enough to hold her new baby. Instead, Fuji held him. Ben's mother was sick so long that Ben thought Fuji was his mother!

One day, Ben's mother tried to hold him. But baby Ben did not know his mother's face or the sound of her voice. He cried when she held him.

He wanted his sister Fuji!

Ben was only a year old when his family moved to another farm several miles away. The new farm was just a mile north of the little town of Hershey, Nebraska.

Ben's brother Fred was born on that second farm not long after the move. Another brother and two sisters were also born there years later. Ben's parents raised their ten children in that tiny, two-bedroom farmhouse.

Many years later, when Ben moved away, he told people he had grown up close to a town named Hershey. People sometimes asked if that was the hometown of Hershey candy bars. Ben told them, "No, it's just a good American town." It was his hometown.

The people of Hershey knew the Kuroki kids as George, Fuji, Cecile, Henry, Wilma, Ben, Fred, Beatrice, Bill, and Rosemary.

Most of the Kuroki children went by both an

American first name and a Japanese middle name. But Ben's sister Fuji just went by her Japanese name.

Ben was the only child in the family who had an American first name and no middle name. His first name was Ben—just Ben—not Benjamin. His full name was just Ben Kuroki, an American-Japanese name for an American boy.

Sam and Naka Kuroki taught all their children to love and respect America. They taught them to work hard and do only good and honorable things. They told their children never to do anything to make the family ashamed.

Honor was an important thing in Japan where Sam and Naka were born. Honor was important in America, too. Ben always remembered that.

Ben always remembered what his dad had told him about his lucky ears, too.

Chapter 4:

Early Farm and School Life

The Kuroki children grew up on the farm near Hershey. The whole family worked hard.

They all helped plow, plant, and harvest the farm and garden crops. They used workhorses and mules. They grew and sold potatoes, wheat, corn, sugar beets, cabbages, carrots, and other foods. They fed chickens and geese and sold eggs. They raised a few cows and milked some of them.

They also raised pigs. The pigs would eat almost anything! The pigs loved to roll around in the mud. That mud kept them from getting sunburned! But, boy, did that mud stink! At least, Ben thought so! Taking care of the pigs was **not** his favorite thing to do on the farm!

The Kuroki family did not have much money. They had to work very hard to feed themselves. A family of twelve ate a lot of food. So did their big farm dog Bruno and all the farm cats!

Farm life was very different in those days. It took many people to do the job by hand. Children had to work as hard as adults did. They often worked from sunrise to sundown, seven days a week. By the time they were fourteen, many boys could easily swing a 100-pound sack of potatoes up onto a wagon or truck.

In those days, farm children were **needed** on the farm. They did chores before and after school. Sometimes they even had to stay home from school to work in the fields. They often missed a lot of school, especially during planting and harvest times.

Ben's mother Naka, a sister, two brothers, and some chickens
and geese on one of the Kuroki family farms

On school days, a school bus drove up to the Kuroki farm. Charley Sullivan, the bus driver, honked his horn. Those children who were going to school rushed to get ready.

Older children helped younger ones. Some tied shoestrings for the others. Some buttoned shirts, coats, or hand-me-down overalls. Some grabbed lunches or homework. Then they ran out and climbed into the bus to ride to the country school.

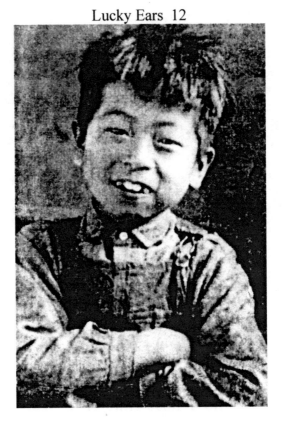

Ben, as a boy, wearing hand-me-down overalls

The Kuroki children brought their lunches to school. Sometimes they brought fish and rice. Often they had only hard biscuits and jam. They had no money for anything else. Their family had food to sell, but they did not have much to eat.

One of Ben's older brothers sometimes rode a

horse to school. At noon, that brother often went to the barn to get his lunch out of his saddlebags. There, he ate his small lunch so no one could watch.

Ben did not say a word for most of his first three months at school. He was always very shy and quiet in class.

Often he knew the answers to the teacher's questions. But when he stood up to answer, he could not speak. He just turned red and stood there until the teacher told him to sit down. Then he wished he could be somewhere else.

Ben was always so quiet in school. No one ever thought he would grow up to be a great speaker!

The only time Ben liked talking at school was during the oral spelling contests. Those contests were also called spelling bees or spelldowns, because if a person misspelled a word, he or she had to sit down. The winner was the last person left standing.   Spelling was one of Ben's best subjects. He could spell almost any word.

Sometimes Ben even went to spelling contests in bigger towns. Once, he went to a state spelling contest. His parents bought him his first suit of clothes for that. They were so proud of him.

On the way to the contest, the car he was in was in an accident. The director of the school was hurt and broke some ribs. But lucky Ben was not hurt.

The country school that Ben and the other Kuroki children attended,
just a mile from the family farm at Hershey, Nebraska

Chapter 5:

Growing Up American

Ben and his brothers and sisters grew up doing things just like other American kids of their time.

They loved to read the cartoons in the Sunday newspapers. The boys wrestled each other to be the first to read those "funny papers." Ben's favorite cartoons were *Little Orphan Annie* and *Popeye.*

In those days, there were no such things as televisions, computers, or video games. Instead, most families had a big radio in their living room.

They gathered around it and listened for news and weather. They also listened just for fun.

Ben and his brothers and sisters really liked to listen to radio stories. They liked mystery, adventure, and funny tales. *Little Orphan Annie* was also one of Ben's favorite radio shows.

But he liked to hear scary programs on the radio, too. Ben often thought about those spooky tales at night when he heard coyotes howl. He tried to forget those scary stories when he walked home alone in the dark from town or after basketball practice!

There were no swimming pools around, so kids then often swam in a pond or an **irrigation** ditch. That was very dangerous! Irrigation water coming out of the ground is very cold—too cold for swimming! Many people have drowned in cold-water ditches like that!

One day, one of Ben's little brothers almost drowned in one. The boys went swimming in the cold-water ditch. They were shivering when one of the older brothers saw four-year-old Bill go underwater. Bill did not come back up. The older brother grabbed little Bill by his hair and pulled him up out of the cold water. He saved Bill's life!

Another time, Ben found another danger. He was outside checking one of his brother's animal traps. As he peered into the dark trap to see if it had caught anything, a skunk shocked him by spraying him right in the eyes! It hurt so much! And Ben could hardly see anything! He was afraid he would be blind forever.

Ben had a hard time finding his way home because he could not see. And when he got there, he really stunk like a skunk! His family would not let him come into the house! They brought out a tub, filled it with water, and made him take a bath outside!

It took a few days before Ben could see well again. He was very happy to be able to see at all!

He knew how lucky he was to get his eyesight back! And he never wanted to see another skunk!

There were many things to do and to watch out for in the country. But there was not much to do in the nearby town of Hershey, except to go to school or to visit friends. It was a small town of only 487 people.

Then, when Ben was about eight, his older brother Henry took Ben and their younger brothers Fred and Bill to North Platte. North Platte was only thirteen miles away—but that seemed so far! And North Platte seemed so much bigger than Hershey!

The bigger town looked so huge to the boys from the country! It had lots more streets than Hershey did! The younger boys were a little bit afraid they would get lost in the bigger town. But they still wanted to look around while older brother Henry went to talk to someone.

While they were there, the sky turned dark

and cloudy. Soon it started to rain. The three younger boys decided to go to the theater to watch a movie and get out of the rain.

Ben and his younger brothers had never seen a movie before. They had never been inside a movie theater. They did not know what to expect.

The movie screen was huge! So were the people on the screen! It was a black and white war movie. In those days, movies were only made in black and white, and most of them had no sound. They were called silent movies.

Ben and his brothers saw a movie called *All Quiet on the Western Front*. It was one of the first movies ever made with sound—very loud sounds!

The movie was about World War I, or the first world war with Germany. Ben and the boys were amazed! As they watched, the sounds of gunfire and war filled the dark theater! It was so noisy! That scared them!

Then it began to rain really hard outside. And

hail began to pound the roof of the theater! It sounded like a real army was fighting a real war right there inside and all around the building!

The boys were afraid. They jumped out of their seats. They ran for the door. They ran out into the rain and hail. They ran down the street. They did not know where they were going. They just ran to get away from the sounds of war.

Their older brother Henry finally found them, a few hours later. They were sitting in a doorway. They were scared, and lost, and wet from the rain!

On the day that Ben first saw that war movie, he had no way of knowing he would fight in a real war someday. He would fight against Germany in World War II or the Second World War.

Later in that war, he would also fight against Japan—where his parents had come from! He would need to be very lucky to survive that war.

But at the time he saw the movie in North Platte, war was nothing to him but a scary movie.

Chapter 6:

Hard Times

Many bad things happened in the U.S. while Ben was growing up. In 1929, he was twelve years old. In that year, the **stock market** crashed. A lot of companies went broke, and people lost their jobs. Life was tough for many years after that.

Many people were suddenly very poor and out of work. When that happens, it is often called a **depression**. The 1930s were so bad, that they were called **The Great Depression**.

The Great Depression was a difficult time in

America. Many people could not pay their bills. Some people lost their homes. Some banks even went out of business.

Other bad things happened, too. The weather turned very bad in Nebraska and in other farming states in the middle of the country. A lot of the food grown in our country comes from there.

Those summers were very hot and dry. Almost no rain fell. That made the ground hard and dry.

Rivers and lakes dried up too. Even the North Platte River went bone dry. A long dry time with no rain is called a **drought**. That two-year drought was the worst in history. Crops dried up. Many farm animals died. Almost nothing grew.

The dry dirt turned to dust. When the wind blew, huge clouds of dust rose up high into the sky. Dirt blew in through the tiny cracks in houses and barns. The few times it did rain, the dirt just turned to mud and then dust.

Everything was dirty. People called the 1930s "the Dirty Thirties" or the "Dust Bowl Days" too.

That was a very bad time for farmers. When things are bad for farmers, the price of food often goes up.

Life was very hard for many people in those days. Lots of them could not pay their bills. They lost their jobs, their money, and their homes or farms. Many people moved away from the farm states to try to find work in towns.

The Kurokis were poor, but they did what they could to pay their bills. Ben picked up glass bottles along the roads. He recycled the bottles and got a few cents for each. He did extra work whenever he could to try to earn money.

So did all his brothers and sisters. Ben's Sister Cecile opened a beauty shop in Hershey. Some of his older brothers and sisters moved to bigger towns to find work.

Ben's oldest brother George was at college in

Lincoln in those days. When their father Sam had a heart attack, George had to drop out of school to take over some of the heavy work on the farm.

Sam got well again. But he and Naka still worried about all their children. They worried about paying their bills and feeding their family.

Sam and Naka Kuroki and 8 of their 10 children at the tiny farmhouse where they lived near Hershey. Ben is the second boy in from the left. The photos of two older sisters are also added at the left.

When Ben was young, men and boys often trapped wild animals for their furs or hides. Ben's brother Henry trapped muskrats and skunks and sold their hides and furs to get money to help the family.

Ben helped in another way. He went hunting with guns. In those days, some people hunted for fun, but most people had even better reasons for hunting. Sometimes they hunted to protect their farm animals from foxes or coyotes or wild dogs. Sometimes they hunted to protect their crops from pests.

Often men and boys hunted deer or other wild animals for food. Especially during the hard times of the 1930s, people sometimes hunted so their families would have enough food to eat. A family could always use a duck, goose, pheasant, deer, or other wild game animal for food.

Of course, hunting is very dangerous! But, in those days, many people grew up using guns. They knew how to use them, so they did not spend a lot of time learning about gun safety. (For safety reasons, today, people often have to get hunting permits or licenses and take classes to learn the safe way to hunt and to handle a gun.)

Ben's best friend was Gordy Jorgenson who lived in Hershey. The two boys really loved to hunt for food and for fun. Some of Gordy's neighbors even gave them extra shotgun shells to take with them. If the boys were lucky, they shot an extra pheasant or duck and brought it back for those friends or neighbors, too.

Ben and Gordy learned about gun safety the hard way. One winter day, they found out just how dangerous guns could be.

That day, they went out to shoot some ducks with their shotguns. Ben was small for his age. His shotgun was so heavy he could hardly lift it.

The boys walked out on the frozen river to get closer to some ducks there. Ben raised his shotgun to shoot at one. He aimed and pulled the trigger.

The heavy shotgun fired, roaring in his ears.

The blast knocked him to the ice. The ice cracked!
He fell through it into very cold water!

His clothes soaked up the river water and
pulled him down! He could not get out! He was
drowning!

Quickly, Gordy got down, flat on the ice,
close to the water. He held out his own empty
shotgun. He told Ben to grab the end of it.

Ben's fingers were so cold! And his clothes
were so heavy with water that he could hardly
raise his arms! Finally, he got his hand out of the
water. His fingers gripped the end of the gun.

Then Gordy pulled as hard as he could! He
pulled his friend out of the water and up onto the
ice! Ben was saved from drowning, but he was
still icy cold!

He was still in danger! Gordy quickly and
carefully started a fire to warm his friend. As soon
as they could, the boys hurried home and got into
dry clothes. It took a long while to get warm. Ben

was very lucky to be alive.

Gordy had saved Ben's life! Ben was very lucky that Gordy had been there to help him and that Gordy had known what to do! After that, the boys almost always went hunting together, and they were always extra careful when using guns or being out in the winter!

Ben always loved to hunt, and he was very good at it. When he was in high school and even after graduation, he often got up at three or four in the morning to go hunting with Gordy. They were excellent hunters.

Those early hunting and survival skills helped feed Ben's family. But those skills also became very important in Ben's life, years later, when he went to fight in the war.

Chapter 7:

The Farm Sale

During the Great Depression of the 1930s, it was very difficult to make a living or to feed a family. The Kurokis did not own their farm. They rented it. During those years, they could not always pay their rent.

They wanted to pay their bills, but they did not have the money. They had always worked very hard, but their farm had never made much money. One day, they could not pay their bills at all.

Over the years, the bank had loaned them

money to buy farm machinery, animals, and seed for their crops. But things had become so bad that few crops and animals were left. Even the farm cats had little to eat and had to be given away.

The family owed money to the bank. They had no way to pay that money back.

Their banker had no choice. He claimed all their property. He held a farm sale to sell everything to pay the bank back for the loans. The Kuroki family was sad and ashamed.

Many people came to the Kuroki farm for the sale. Most of them were friends and neighbors. None of them had much money to spend or to lend to their friends.

The neighbors and friends did not come to buy things at the sale. They came to show support and respect for their friends, the Kuroki family.

The bank tried to sell everything at the farm sale, but no one bought much. Few people had any money. And no one wanted to take the things that belonged to the Kurokis!

At the end of the sale, no one had bought the farm, so the banker let the Kurokis stay there.

Then some of their friends got together. They loaned Sam Kuroki a little money. He used it to buy back his workhorses and some of his machinery.

In that way, the family was able to keep farming. Sam and Naka were happy. They could start over on their farm.

All his life, Ben and his family were very thankful for what happened that day. They had many friends and neighbors who helped them. Ben always said they were very lucky to have such good friends in Nebraska.

Ben's mom and dad said so, too. They never went back to their native Japan even though their children would have paid their way there to visit relatives.

Ben, Gordy, and Ben's younger brother Fred were all on
the Hershey High School basketball team.

Chapter 8:

Better Times

In the mid-1930s, Ben was still living on the farm with his parents and his younger brothers and sisters. He did farm work and went to high school in the town of Hershey when he could.

Ben was good at class work, but he thought the best thing about school was just being with his pals. He especially liked being with his best friends Gordy Jorgenson and Bill Dymond, and his brother Fred. The boys loved to play sports.

Ben's school in town did not have a football team, but he and his friends played other sports.

Ben loved to play basketball, baseball, softball, and tennis. He also loved to run track with the other boys!

Sometimes they played ball at school or at a friend's house until long after dark. Sometimes they liked to wrestle or climb around in the barn instead.

Those were good times. Ben and his family did not have much money, but he was lucky. He had a lot of good friends, especially in school.

Ben was popular in school, too. In his last two years of high school, his class elected him vice president. His best friend Gordy was elected president of the class all four years.

But Ben worried he might not be able to graduate with Gordy and their class. Living in the country and working on the farm, he had missed a lot of school.

Ben also worried that he had not learned as much in school as his town classmates had. He knew he needed to work very hard to catch up on all his high school classwork. Graduation time was coming soon.

School picture of Ben Kuroki, Vice President of his
Senior Class in High School

In 1936, Gordy and more than a dozen classmates all graduated from high school together. Ben was one of them. He knew he was very lucky to be able to graduate after missing so much school! After graduation, he continued to work on the family farm.

By then, other good things were starting to happen again in America. Rain brought water to the rivers and fields. Farmers planted and harvested more crops. People began to make a little more money.

Life was getting better in the United States. The drought, the Dirty Thirties, the Dust Bowl Days, and The Great Depression were almost over.

By the time Ben was twenty, things were changing on the farms too. Farming was still very hard. But farmers were starting to use new kinds of machines, like tractors. The new machines helped make life a little easier.

Farmers also hauled their products to markets further away from home. Ben's family bought a big truck and trailer. Ben and a man named Max began to take farm products across the state.

But things did not always go well.   Farm trucks like that were heavy and very hard to handle.   On their first trip, Ben and Max took a truckload of cabbages to Omaha.

They drove down a big hill onto a busy street there.   Just then, a car turned right in front of them. Max tried not to hit the car, but he turned the truck too sharply. The truck pulled to the side of the road and almost rolled over.

Hundreds of cabbages spilled out of the truck. The cabbages rolled all over the street, like dodge balls on a basketball court. A newspaper ran a picture of the accident on its front page! Luckily, Ben and Max were not hurt.

On their third long truck trip, another bad thing happened. Max fell asleep while driving. This time, the truck rolled into the ditch. Max was not hurt, but Ben went through the glass and cut his arm.   He was very lucky not to be hurt too badly. But the truck was ruined!

Ben's family bought a new truck and a special trailer that kept things cool. Then, Ben and another man started taking fruits and vegetables across the country. They made a little more money from those longer trips.

In between trips, Ben sometimes visited Gordy and his family. By then, Gordy was married, and he ran a gas station in town.

Ben and Gordy were still good friends. They did things together when they could. They still went hunting now and then.

Ben had many other friends in the area, too. Some of them were also Japanese Americans. On Sundays, Ben played on a Japanese-American baseball team. They called their team the Nisei Cubs. The word **Nisei** (or second generation) means Japanese-American people born in America to parents who were born in Japan.

Ben liked sports, but he knew he would never

be a sports star. He was not big enough.

The Nisei Cubs—Ben and his Japanese-American baseball team
from the Hershey/North Platte, Nebraska, area

Ben did not yet know what he wanted to do with the rest of his life. He knew he did not want to be a farmer or a trucker, but he had not yet found the right job for himself. He only knew that he wanted to be lucky enough to amount to something good.

World War II MAP – Japan, United States, Germany

This map shows that during World War II, the United States,
England, and other countries were fighting against both
Germany and Japan (and many other countries)
across at least two different oceans.

Chapter 9:

War!

When Ben was twenty-one, life was a little better on the farm. But very scary things were happening in other parts of the world.

Ben and his family often listened to the radio. They heard about a new war going on in Europe.

They heard about a man named Adolf Hitler in Germany. They heard how Hitler wanted to take over most of Europe. They were afraid America would soon be at war with Germany—as in that World War I movie Ben and his younger brothers had seen in the North Platte theater years before.

They also heard and read news about another war in Japan. Japan is in Asia. That was where Ben's parents came from and where they were born. The news said Japan wanted to take over a huge country called China.

It sounded like the whole world might soon be at war again, a World War II. Many Americans did not want to go to war with Germany or Japan. Many Americans wanted to stay out of war.

But this time, it really sounded like Japan would be an enemy, too, if America went to war. Ben's family worried about that!

In Nebraska, Ben had never had a problem being Japanese American. He was an American! He was a Nebraskan! People there did not care that he looked Japanese.

But many people were worried about war. They worried about other people who might be their enemies. They worried about people in America who might be Japanese or German.

One day, Ben faced that kind of trouble in another state. People there became angry when they saw the Kuroki name on his truck. They knew it was a Japanese name. Ben was afraid someone might try to hurt him or his truck just because his name was Japanese.

Ben's Japanese-American friends worried, too. They worried war would come to America. They worried their families might get caught up in the war. They did not know what to do.

One day, about twenty of them met in the basement of a church in North Platte to talk about what to do. During that meeting, the police came and took one of the visiting men away. No one knew what was happening.

After the meeting, someone told them the war had started—war with Japan! The Japanese Americans were very afraid. What had happened, and why? What would happen to their families?

The day of that meeting was December 7,

1941. On that day, Japanese planes had attacked a place called Pearl Harbor.

Pearl Harbor was the name of an American military base. That base was on the island of Hawaii. Hawaii was not yet a state. It was just a group of islands protected by the U.S.A.

Many American ships and planes were destroyed at Pearl Harbor that day. They were bombed by Japanese planes. Many American sailors died there.

Because of that attack, the United States went to war against Japan. Soon after that, Germany declared war on America, too. The world was at war—World War II.

Ben and three of his brothers would later join the military. They would become American soldiers in that war against Japan and Germany. They would all be lucky. They would all come back alive! Other men would not be so lucky.

Chapter 10:

Joining the Army

Ben's father Sam was very angry. Japan—the country where Sam had been born—had attacked his new country—the United States of America.

Sam believed the Japanese had made a sneak attack on Pearl Harbor. He said the attack was not an honorable thing for Japan to do. That made Sam ashamed and very angry at Japan.

After the attack, America declared war on Japan, too. Sam knew the war would bring many problems. He worried about his family and his friends.

Sam told his middle sons Ben and Fred that Japan was now their enemy. He said they had to prove they were American, not Japanese. He told them they had to join the American Army and go to war. It was their duty.

Ben and Fred agreed. They truly wanted to fight for their country—their America!

Ben and Fred drove to North Platte to try to join the Army. (Many stories about Ben mistakenly say that he first tried to get into the Army in Grand Island. Ben always said he tried to join in North Platte first. It was closer to his home.)

Ben and Fred went to the Army doctor at North Platte. The doctor told them they were healthy enough to be soldiers. They signed the papers to join the Army. Then the Army told them to go home and wait.

Ben and Fred went home. They were proud and happy. They told everyone they would soon be in the Army, just like many of their friends. They thought they would soon be fighting for their country—the United States of America.

Every day, friends asked Ben and Fred when they would leave to go to war. They wondered, too. Some of their friends and neighbors had already gone to war.

Ben and Fred waited almost two weeks, but the Army did not call them. Finally, they called the Army.

They found out that the Army did not want them. Ben and Fred were Americans who looked Japanese. Their last name was Japanese. The American Army was fighting the Japanese Army. The government did not know what to do with them.

The boys were embarrassed and angry. They felt it was their duty to fight for their country— America!

Then, days later, Ben heard something on the

radio. It said the **Army Air Corps** needed men.
That word **corps** sounded just like the word core,
but it meant group.

At that time, the Air Corps was a new part of
the Army—an army of airplanes and their crews.
Early in that war, the Air Corps was just a part of
the Army. (Later, the Air Corps became a separate
group. Its name was then changed to the Air
Force.)

The radio said the Army wanted men to join
their new Air Corps or Air Force. It said that men
could come to Grand Island and join there.

Ben liked planes. He had even taken lessons
to learn to fly. And he wanted to join the Army!
But he worried the Air Corps would not take him.
The Army had not wanted him. Would the new
Army Air Corps want him?

Grand Island was a long way from Hershey—
150 miles away! It would be a long drive to Grand
Island just to try to join the Army Air Corps. It

would be an even longer trip if the Air Corps did not want him!

Ben decided to phone the Army office in Grand Island to ask them if they would let him join. He talked to the man who signed up the soldiers. Ben asked the man if he cared who he signed up. Did he worry about a man's name? Did it matter what a man looked like or where his family came from?

The Army man thought about Ben's questions. He said, "No, I get $2.00 for every man I sign up. I don't care who he is."

Ben was delighted. He and Fred drove to Grand Island. There, they gave their pledge of allegiance and joined the Army Air Corps.

Someone took their picture and put it on the front page of the *Omaha World-Herald* newspaper! Ben and Fred were so happy. At last, they were going to fight for their country.

...But even that would not be easy. They

would have to fight very hard for the right to be American soldiers.   And they would need to be very lucky just to stay in the Army.

Chapter 11:

Army Training

Ben and Fred soon left for Army Air Corps training. Buses, trains, and trucks took them far away to bases in Kansas, Texas, and other states. They were very proud and a little afraid.

Back in Nebraska, they had been treated just like anyone else. They had many friends. They were Americans. It did not matter that they looked Japanese.

But, on the road, they soon found themselves among strangers who did not like them. Ben and Fred looked Japanese. And other people often treated them like they **were** Japanese!

Many people looked at them with fear or anger—as if they were the enemy. Some people called them names or tried to make them fight. But others just ignored them. When someone was nice to them, other people got angry.

While they traveled, Ben and Fred tried to be very quiet. They tried not to call attention to themselves. That was hard, not being able to talk to each other. They could not help looking different. They could not help looking like the enemy.

At the training bases, they met men from all over the country. They learned to fight and shoot like soldiers. They learned to follow orders. They learned how to work like a team in the Army.

While the other men learned more about that, Ben and Fred were ordered to do other things. They often worked in a kitchen. They peeled potatoes and washed dishes for many days or even weeks at a time.

They had to do the jobs no one else wanted to do! At first, Ben and Fred did not mind. Later, they felt like they were being punished just for looking different.

They knew the Army wanted them to quit and go home. They would not do that! They wanted to prove they were just as American as anyone else. They wanted to fight for their country!

Then, after only two weeks on an Army air base in Texas, Fred was kicked out of the Air Corps. He did not know why. He was sent back to the Army to dig ditches. Fred did not want to leave the Air Corps or his brother, but he had no choice.

Ben was on duty and was shocked to find out his brother had left. They did not even get a chance to say good-bye to each other.

After Fred left, Ben felt hurt, lonely, and sad. He missed his brother. He wondered why Fred had to leave. He wondered why he was able to stay. For the first time, Ben wondered if the lucky holes in his ears had something to do with it. Maybe they really were lucky—for him.

Ben's brother Fred in his Army uniform during the war

Chapter 12:

Waiting to Go to War

Ben was still afraid the Air Corps would make him leave. He did not want to be sent away, like his brother had been. He would do anything to stay. If he had to beg to stay in the Air Corps, he would do that!

But it would not be easy. Ben often heard rumors that he was being sent away. Each time he heard that, he went to tell his story and to beg to stay. One officer listened and helped him. His name was Lieutenant Charles Brannan.

Ben also made friends with another soldier

named Al Kuhn. The two of them took Army classes together. They graduated from Army Air Corps school at the same time.

One day, Ben and Al were riding in a truck with more than a dozen other soldiers. The driver turned the truck too sharply. It went off the road and flipped over.

Al broke some of his ribs. Most of the men in the truck were hurt. But Ben was not hurt at all. He did not even get a scratch on him!

Ben went to see Al in the hospital. There, he told Al about his lucky ears. Ben said his ears had saved him. He showed Al the tiny holes in his lucky ears. Al laughed so hard that his ribs hurt.

When Al was well, he and Ben were sent to another air base. There, Ben saw his first B-24 airplane. It was a big shiny bomber—the biggest, most beautiful plane he had ever seen.

Ben could hardly wait to fly in one! He knew he would never be a pilot, but he still hoped he could be a crewman on a B-24!

Instead, the Air Corps sent him to work in the kitchen again. There he heard he was going to be sent away to another part of the Army, like his brother Fred had been.

Ben went to see Lieutenant Brannan again to ask for his help. Ben wanted to fight the enemy. He begged to fight for his country. With tears in his eyes, he begged to stay in the Air Corps. Then he waited to see what would happen.

Again, Lieutenant Brannan told him he could stay. Ben felt that was the biggest break of his Army career.

Soon, Ben and Al heard that they were going to be sent to war, across the ocean. The Army gave them ten free days to go home and see their families before going to war.

Ben's family was fine. But Ben heard that many Japanese Americans were not doing so well. They had been sent away from their homes with only those things they could carry. Many of them had lost almost everything they owned. They were sent to live in dusty camps behind barbed wire fences. Those places were called **internment camps**.

Those Japanese Americans were put there so they would not help the Japanese—the enemy. But the people in the camps were not Japanese. They were Americans who looked Japanese.

Ben did not think that was right. But it was wartime, and things were different. People in America were afraid of anyone who might be Japanese or German.

Ben's family was lucky. They were never sent away to such a camp. They did not lose their home or the other things they owned. They still had many friends.

While Ben was home for his visit, he went to see Gordy's family and other friends. Gordy and his wife had had a baby. Gordy was not home. He was in the military, too. Ben missed seeing him.

Gordy in his military uniform

After his visit home, Ben went back to his Air
Corps base. He and Al waited for a ship to take
them to war. Ben was going to fight the enemy!
His good luck was back. He was on his way to a
base in England!

This map shows where the war with Germany was fought during
World War II, including Germany, North Africa (Morocco,
Algeria, Tunisia, and Libya), Romania (Ploesti raid),
England, and other lands and water areas.

Chapter 13:

Lucky to Be a Gunner

Ben was part of the first B-24 bomber group in England. But he was not allowed to fly. The Air Corps gave him a desk job instead, but they gave him no work to do. All he could do was watch the other men in his group fly off in their planes.

Ben dreamed of flying in a B-24. Each plane needed four or five gunners, as well as other crewmen. Ben asked what he could do to become a gunner on one of the planes. But no one had an answer for him.

Then one day Ben got his chance—another lucky break. A pilot named Jake Epting came to talk to him. One of Jake's gunners had lost some fingers to **frostbite**. Jake asked if Ben would take the gunner's place on his plane. The pilot felt Ben would be a good gunner.

Before Jake even talked to Ben, he had asked his crew if they would fly with a man who looked Japanese—like the enemy. The men in his crew said that a man's looks did not matter. They wanted the best gunners on their plane. If Ben could do a good job as a gunner, then he was welcome.

Ben would prove to be an excellent gunner. He would become an important part of the crew. He would take turns manning the guns anywhere in the plane. He would work wherever he was needed.

As a gunner, Ben would sit in one of the clear plastic-like bubbles on the plane. Each bubble was like a rounded window. The bubbles let the gunner see out. The big bubbles were on top, at the rear, on the sides, and on the underside of the plane. Each bubble was called a **turret** or a **canopy**.

Each gunner had one to two big machine guns in his turret. The guns could be moved up and down and side to side, so the gunner could shoot at any planes coming at him.

The gunner always kept his eyes open. He watched for attacks from enemy planes.

The clear turret made it easy for the gunner to see the enemy. But the enemy could also see him! There was also no heat in that part of the plane. The turret was a very cold and scary place to be.

If a gunner was good at his job, and if he was very lucky, his plane and crew might make it through the war. Ben hoped to be a very good gunner—and a very lucky one.

Ben (in front) and three of his B-24 crew members

Chapter 14:

War in the Desert

Ben's B-24 group was going to a new base, but they did not know where. They might be sent to Germany, or Japan, or somewhere else. Ben wanted to go to war against Japan. But it was not his choice to make.

One day the men got their orders. They were not going to war against Japan. They were going to war against Germany. They were going to North Africa to do that.

Ben was disappointed. He was not going to fight against Japan. But he could still fight for his country!

His crew's first real bombing mission was in North Africa. The crew worried about the date—the 13th of the month. That did not sound like a lucky day!

The first part of their mission went well. Then, suddenly, an explosion rocked their big B-24 bomber.

The tail gunner was a man named Dawley. A piece of metal tore into the turret where Dawley was. It hit him in the head. It knocked him out.

The crew pulled Dawley into the belly of the plane to help him. He was hurt very badly, and his head was bleeding. One of the crewmen grabbed a first-aid kit. He bent down to give Dawley a shot to kill his pain.

Ben saw what was happening. Then he remembered something he had learned in Army school: **Do not give medicine to a man with a head wound if the man is not awake!** Ben knew the shot could kill Dawley!

Ben had to stop the crewman from giving Dawley the shot! It was noisy in the plane, but Ben finally made the man understand him! The man put the shot away. Then the crew covered Dawley with a blanket to keep him warm.

When the plane landed, the crew took Dawley to the hospital. He did not wake up for four days! The doctor said Ben had saved the man's life. Dawley was very lucky Ben was on that plane!

But Ben was also lucky. He took over as tail gunner in Dawley's place.

That tail gunner space was very small and very cold. But Ben did not complain. He was glad to be able to fly in the plane and to fight for his country.

Ben and his crew only needed to make it through 25 missions. Then they could go home.

Ben's crew spent their first Christmas together in the desert. They flew many missions after that. They became good friends. His pilot even gave him a very special nickname. He said Ben was a "Most Honorable Son" of America.

Before long, Ben was raised in rank to technical sergeant. He felt like a very lucky man.

The Running Panda Bear Patch
(a bear carrying a bomb) (as seen on Ben's jacket on pages vi and 79)
was worn by the crew members of Ben's 93rd Bomb Group of B-24s.
The 93rd Bomb Group was commanded by General "Ted" Timberlake
and was sometimes called "Ted Timberlake's Traveling Circus"
because the men and planes flew so many missions over
so many different countries during World War II.

Chapter 15:

Captured!

Ben's crew flew more missions. Then, for their second Christmas, they were sent back to England. But while they were flying over the desert, something went wrong.

Their plane got lost somewhere over North Africa. It ran out of gas. Luckily, Captain Jake Epting was able to land the plane safely.

Suddenly, several men came running toward the downed plane. They were natives. They yelled and waved guns, knives, and clubs at the men in the airplane.

Then more men rode up on horses. Those new men were soldiers from Spain. They chased the natives away. They captured the crew and took them to a nearby town.

Their leader kept asking if Ben was from Japan. He could not understand why Ben looked Japanese or why he was fighting for America.

The Spanish men locked Ben's crew in a nearby building. Their leader told the crew that the war was over for them. He said they would spend the rest of the war in prison.

But they were lucky. Ben's plane had landed in a country controlled by Spain. Spain was **neutral**. That meant Spain was neither a friend nor an enemy of America or of Germany. That was good news.

The next day, Ben's crew heard the bad news. The natives had found some German things in the plane—things the crewmen had found or bought. But the natives thought the crewmen were spies. If

An American B-24 bomber flying through machine gunfire and heavy
smoke and fire. This was during a low-level bombing run on German
oilfields at Ploesti, Romania. The B-24s had flown for more than six
hours from North Africa, over the Mediterranean Sea, and into
enemy territory in Europe. The surviving planes then flew
more than six hours back to their bases in North Africa.

Enemy machine guns shot at them from the
ground and from train cars. Enemy planes flew all
around, shooting at them. Explosions lit up the
sky and rocked the planes in the air. Some planes
crashed around them.

Ben's crew dropped bombs on the oilfield.

Then they turned around and started back on the long trip home!

Ben's plane was the first one to land back at their base. Then he and his crew waited for the other planes to come back. Of the nine planes in their small group, only two returned—Ben's plane and one other.

In all, at least 52 of the 178 planes were lost or shot down. More than 300 American airmen died that day! Ben said that mission was the most frightening and toughest of all the ones he ever flew. But that raid helped slow down the German Army.

Ploesti was Ben's 24th mission. Most of the men in Ben's crew had finished their 25th mission and had gone home. Ben had been the last man to join his crew. He had just one more mission to fly to make his 25th. Then he could go home, too. But he wanted to do more. So, he signed up to do five more missions!

Ben said the extra missions were for America. They were for his brothers who could not serve in the Air Corps. They were for the Japanese-American people in internment camps. And they were for Americans of different races, religions, and skin colors. Ben was still at war against the enemies of his country. He was also at war against racism.

His old crew had gone home. So Ben found himself with a brand new crew. The new men had very little experience and lots of bad luck.

On his 30th and last mission with them, Ben sat in the gunner's place at the top of the plane. The flight started out very calmly.

Below him in the plane was the radio room. Sometimes the man in the radio room became bored. Sometimes that man reached up and pulled the pant leg of the gunner in the turret above him. He did that to see if the gunner was awake. Or sometimes he did that just to talk to the gunner.

On that 30th mission, the radio man pulled Ben's pant leg. Ben bent down to see what the other man wanted.

Suddenly, something hit the plastic-like bubble above Ben! It exploded! The force knocked Ben out. The radio man quickly pulled Ben down into the belly of the plane. Ben was knocked out, but he was alive and unhurt. He was not even scratched! His lucky ears were still protecting him!

When the plane landed, the crew looked at the hole in the plastic bubble. They could not believe their eyes. They removed the glass-like canopy. Ben held it over his head. He put his head through the hole. Someone took a picture.

The radio man had accidentally saved Ben's life! If Ben had been sitting up straight at the time of the explosion, he would have been killed! Lucky Ben and his special ears had been lucky one more time!

Ben with his head sticking up through the hole in the glass-like canopy
(notice the running panda bear patch on his jacket)

Ben finished his 30 missions—five more than most airmen would ever have. Ben was lucky. He was alive. He was going home, and he was grateful that he had survived!

Ben saying goodbye to some of his B-24 crewmates
as he prepares to go home

Chapter 17:

Home

Ben earned many medals and honors. He received some of those medals quietly. The rest of his crew received theirs during a big ceremony while Ben sat alone in another building. He felt hurt and wondered why he was not with them.

Ben came home to America. He got a hero's welcome of his own. His picture and story showed up in newspapers and magazines all across America. He talked on many radio shows.

But Ben was not a hero to everyone. Some people still looked at him as if he were just

Japanese, not Japanese American. They treated him as if he were the enemy. In some towns, he could not get a taxi cab, or a hotel room, or even a haircut.

The Army sent Ben to a California beach hotel for a rest. He was invited to be on a national radio program. But when he got there, he was told he could not be on the show. Many people in California did not like the Japanese. They did not even like a Japanese-American war hero.

A few days later, Ben spoke to a big group in California. It was called the Commonwealth Club of San Francisco. The people in that club had heard speeches from every American president since Abraham Lincoln.

When Ben got to the Club, he saw angry people carrying signs outside the building. He was afraid to walk the streets in an Army **uniform**. He was afraid the people in the club might boo him or start fights. He wanted to cancel the speech, but it was too late.

Ben's hands shook as he gave the first words of his speech. He said, "I'm just a farm boy from Nebraska. I can't speak for all soldiers, but I can speak for myself." He then talked about honor and duty, about friendship and patriotism, about the brotherhood of soldiers, and about being an American.

When he finished talking, all 600 people in the room stood up. They clapped for him for such a long time that he had to return to the stage two more times to say a few more words. Many of those people had tears in their eyes. (Some of them would later help Ben when he tried to get permission to fly against Japan during the war.)

Magazines and newspapers printed his speech. People wrote letters to him. Many of them said Ben's speech was a turning point in the war. It helped other Americans start to like Japanese Americans. Ben thought giving that speech was one of the most important things he ever did during the war.

Then Ben ran into a soldier friend named Eddie Bates. Eddie's brother had been killed by the Japanese during the war. Ben wanted to do something for his friend and for others. Ben wanted to go back and fight the Japanese, too. But how could he go back to war again?

Someone told Ben to talk to Colonel Warren Williams of the Army Air Corps. Ben wrote to him. Before long, the Air Force sent Ben to a B-29 bomber base in Kansas.

At first, Ben was excited. But the longer he waited, the more he worried. Nothing seemed to be happening.

While Ben waited to go back to war, the Army sent him to talk at three internment camps around the country. Many Japanese Americans were forced to live in those camps. They lived in poor housing behind barbed wire.

The Army wanted Ben to talk to the people living in those camps. The Army wanted him to urge the young men there to join the **442nd Infantry Regiment** of Japanese Americans, to fight as soldiers for their country—America.

Ben felt uncomfortable in the camps, inside the barbed wire fences. The guards at the camps wore uniforms like his, but they did not look like him. The people living inside the camps looked a lot more like he did.

Many of the younger people in the camps looked at Ben as if he was a movie star. He was 25 years old. He was 5'9" tall and weighed 150 pounds. He did not look like an American movie star. But he was a war hero—and he looked a lot like they did. That made him very special to them.

Ben was also a Nisei, like they were. The young Nisei people in the camps wanted to talk to him and touch him. They listened to every word he said. They wanted his autograph.

Ben signing autographs for young Japanese Americans
at an internment camp

Ben surrounded by young Japanese Americans at an internment camp

Ben became a real hero to some of those young people. Many young Nisei men joined the 442nd Regiment of the Army because of him. Many of those Japanese-American soldiers won honors and awards. Those men won more medals in the war than any other group.

Ben speaking at one of the internment camps
(note the Nisei in uniform on stage at the right)

But Ben was not a hero to some of the older

Japanese-American people. Many of them had lost everything they owned—everything they had worked so hard for. Those people did not like what America had done to their families. They did not like Ben at all.

Ben could not stop thinking about his own family. They were lucky. They were safe back in Nebraska.

If he had grown up in such a camp, would he have wanted to fight for America? He did not know. Still it bothered him to see guards dressed in uniforms pointing guns at people who looked like him.

Chapter 18:

Another War

While Ben was visiting the camps, he received a very sad letter from his sister Cecile. It read, "So sorry to give you the bad news. Gordy has been killed in the Solomon Islands."

Ben was heartbroken. His best friend had been killed by the Japanese. He went to see Gordy's Mom and Dad, and he cried.

Then he did not know what to do! All he knew was that he **had** to go to war again. He had to fight the Japanese for Gordy, his own family, Eddie Bates' brother, and America.

Ben called Colonel Williams and told him the story. Before long, the Air Corps sent Ben back to Nebraska, to a B-29 bomber base at Harvard, near Hastings.

Ben became the tail gunner on a huge B-29 plane. The B-29 was the biggest plane in the war. It was much bigger than his old B-24 bomber. Some of those B-29s were even made by the Glenn Martin Company near Omaha, in Nebraska.

Ben's new pilot was James Jenkins, and his crew got along well. The men heard they were going to war against Japan! Ben and his crew were ready.

Then, not long before they were to leave, Ben heard about a new ruling. It said no Japanese American could fly against Japan. Ben's pilot argued against the rule, but it did no good. Ben could not fly against Japan!

Ben looked for people who could help him. He wrote many letters to Colonel Williams. He also talked to a Nebraska **politician** named Carl Curtis. **Congressman** Curtis sent a message to General Marshall. Then Ben sent letters to some of his new friends in California. At least three of those important men from California sent messages to the U.S. War Department.

Soon Ben got a letter from a man named Henry Stimson. He was the Secretary of War for the United States! The Stimson letter said that the new ruling did not apply to Ben Kuroki. Ben could fly in the war against Japan, along with his B-29 crew!

Ben's big B-29 bomber was fully loaded and ready to take off. The engines were turning. Most of the crew was onboard—but not the pilot.

Suddenly, Ben's pilot rushed up to the plane. He asked Ben for the Stimson letter. Ben dug it out of his bag and handed it to Jenkins who ran off with it.

Ben was worried! What was happening this

time? Why had the pilot taken his letter?

Then someone told Ben that the pilot had been ordered not to fly with Ben on the plane. The pilot had taken his letter to show that the new ruling did not apply to Ben Kuroki.

Soon Jenkins ran back to the plane. He had a smile on his face. He had the Stimson letter in his hand. Everyone got ready. Quickly, the plane flew off to war against Japan—before anyone could stop it again.

Once again, luck was riding with Ben and his lucky ears. Ben would fly against the Japanese. He would be the only Japanese-American gunner to fly in a B-29 against Japan during World War II. He would also be the only Japanese-American to fly against **both** Japan and Germany during that war.

Ben's B-29 crew was very proud to have him onboard. They were so proud they named their plane "The Honorable Sad Saki" for him.

Pilot James Jenkins and Sergeant Ben Kuroki at the nosewheel
of their B-29 bomber "The Honorable Sad Saki"

Here is where the name Sad Saki came from:

"Sad Sack" was the name of an American cartoon

soldier. Saki (pronounced like sock-ee) was a Japanese drink. Ben's crew combined those terms with a word of respect to make "The Honorable Sad Saki" or one of the many nicknames they sometimes called Ben.

Ben's B-29 crew in front of their airplane "The Honorable Sad Saki"—
a plane named for one of Ben's nicknames

Chapter 19:

War in the Pacific

Ben's plane and crew were sent to an air base on Tinian. That was a tiny island way out in the Pacific Ocean. From there, Ben would finally fight against Japan, but the island was not a safe place for him.

At times, Japanese soldiers hid out on the island. Sometimes they dressed up in stolen American uniforms and shot at the U.S. soldiers. Americans on the island were told to shoot anyone who looked Japanese. Ben looked Japanese. He was in danger—even from his own Army!

Ben and his crew worried that American

soldiers would shoot him. When he needed to go anywhere, some of his crew walked beside him. They tried hard to protect him. But they could not be with him every minute.

Ben worried that the Japanese might take him prisoner. What would they do to a Japanese-American soldier? Would they shoot him or beat him to death?

Ben and his crew flew many missions from that island. Many of those missions were right over Japan. Ben worried that his plane would crash there. He worried that he would be captured.

He did not sleep well at night on that island. He often had terrible nightmares that kept him awake. He was very tired and worried. The Army Air Force was worried about him, too.

The Army said he had done enough. He had already flown a total of 40 missions—that was 30 against Germany and 10 more against Japan. That was far more than most airmen had done. He could go home and teach other airmen to be gunners.

But Ben said no! He had worked too hard to get where he was. He had a job to finish! He just needed to go somewhere safe and rest for a few days. The Air Force agreed. They sent his crew to Hawaii for one week's rest. When he came back, he was ready to fly again.

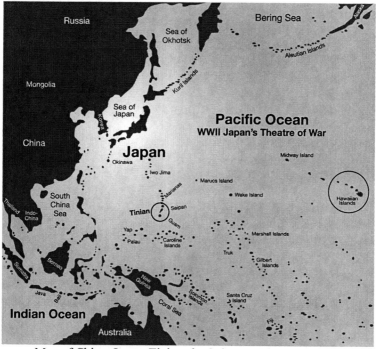

Map of China, Japan, Tinian, the Solomon Islands, Hawaii, and other Areas in the Pacific Ocean

Ben flew 28 missions against Japan with his crew. On the day he landed after his 58th mission, he and some of his crew went to have a drink and play cards to relax.

One of the crewmen drank too much. He was a very big man, and he was very drunk. He started to argue with Ben about which of them was more patriotic.

Ben was a quiet man, but he was also very patriotic. He had worked very hard to earn the right to fight for his country. He had flown in more missions than any of the other crewmen.

Ben felt he had proven his love for America. He would not let anyone question his patriotism. He would not back down.

But the other man was very drunk and very angry. He pulled out a big knife. He stabbed Ben in the top of his head.

Another crewman, Sergeant Russell Olsen, probably saved Ben's life. He stepped between

Ben and the man with the knife. He protected Ben until the ambulance came and took him to the hospital.

The doctors put 24 stitches in Ben's head. He was lucky. If the knife had cut just a little deeper, he would have died.

Ben was still in the hospital when he heard some good news. World War II was over! Japan had surrendered after two major cities in Japan were hit with atomic bombs. America had won.

Ben had flown 58 missions. It was a miracle he had survived. He did not need to do any more.

The man who had stabbed Ben was in jail. The rest of Ben's crew flew their plane back home to the United States in just a few days. They flew home to America without him.

Ben had to stay in the hospital many days, but he was lucky. He had survived the war.

Sergeant Ben Kuroki, standing in front of
a "Nisei-American" poster during the war

Chapter 20:

Home Again

Messages were slow in those days. The Army expected Ben to come back to America with his crew. The Army had special plans for him. They wanted him to speak at another important meeting.

But Ben was not on the plane. At first, the Army did not know where he was. They did not know he was in the hospital back on the island.

Ben came back to America as soon as he could. He came home on a very slow ship. It took 21 days before he was finally back in America.

By the time the ship landed, Ben had been in

the same clothes for many days. His uniform was sweaty and dirty. His shoes needed to be polished. He had not shaved for days. He was a mess, and he knew it! But there was no place to get clean— and he only had a nickel in his pocket!

A man was waiting for Ben to get off the ship. The man took Ben to a fancy hotel in New York.

Ben went in the back door of the hotel. He found his way to the main desk. No one knew him there. The fancy guests turned up their noses at his dirty clothes.

But things changed when people found out Ben was there to meet someone from a big New York newspaper. Suddenly, Ben had his own hotel room!

Ben was only a sergeant. The other speakers were General Marshall and two other Army generals. All of them were to speak at that big newspaper's yearly meeting the next day.

A famous writer named Millard Lampell

helped Ben write his speech. Lampell had written a radio play about Ben, called "The Boy From Nebraska." The two men had written to each other but had never met before.

Ben's clothes were still dirty. He had no way to wash them. He knew he could not make an important speech looking like that. He sent a message to his brother George asking for money.

George sent Ben money to get his clothes cleaned and his shoes shined. Ben also got a haircut and a shave. Then he was ready.

Ben's speech was a big success. The Army sent him on a tour of the country. He gave more speeches and talked on radio shows. A famous artist painted a picture of him for an art museum in Washington D.C. The artist also gave him a second painting of himself for his parents.

A writer named Ralph Martin wrote a book about him called *Boy From Nebraska*. Someone even included a story about Ben in a comic book about real true heroes and the war.

Ben had fought hard for the right to fight for his country—America. He had earned medals, but he still could not get a hotel room or a taxi cab in some towns. That did not seem fair to him.

Many other people were good American citizens, too. It did not matter what color or religion they were. Ben thought that all good American citizens deserved to be treated fairly.

Ben decided that he needed to speak for all American citizens. That would be his last mission—his 59th mission!

Ben began his own speaking tour across the country. He talked about his 59th mission—fair treatment for all good American citizens. He spoke in schools, at clubs, and at all kinds of meetings. His story was retold on the radio and in newspapers and magazines.

While on one speaking tour, Ben stopped in Utah to see some friends. There, he met a girl named Shige Tanabe. Ben had finally met the girl for him—a Japanese-American girl!

But there was a problem. Ben only had a high school education. Shige was in college. Her parents were educated. They thought education was very important. They would not let their daughter marry Ben until he promised to graduate from college. Ben promised.

Ben and Shige married. They moved back to Nebraska. He started school at the University of Nebraska in Lincoln. That school was also one of only three colleges in the country to accept Japanese Americans from the internment camps as students in those days.

Ben decided to take college classes to become a newspaperman. In his spare time, he sometimes worked for his good friend Cal Stewart. Stewart was a Nebraska newspaperman, too. He had been in Ben's Air Force group in England.

Ben worked hard in school. He graduated

from college with a **journalism** or news writing degree in just three years! Then he and Shige bought a weekly newspaper business in York, Nebraska.

Other newspaper people heard about Ben. Many of them came to help him put out his first newspaper. It was a great success. That paper was usually only eight pages long, but his first one was 40 pages!

A year later, a flood destroyed Ben's business. His friends helped him rebuild. But it took too long, and things did not go well. Ben finally sold the newspaper. He went to work for other newspapers in Nebraska and Idaho.

Then he bought a weekly newspaper in Michigan. He and Shige moved their young family there. Ten years later, they moved to California. Ben went to work at a daily newspaper in Ventura, until he retired in 1984. He and his wife then lived in Camarillo, California.

In 1999, when Ben was 82, he found out he needed heart surgery. A week later, his wife Shige did, too. They both had major heart surgery within days of each other. At that time, an important part of Ben's heart was replaced with part of a cow's heart! That meant he had more lucky years with his lucky ears.

After retiring, Ben still kept busy. He loved being with his family. He still gave speeches about fair treatment for all American citizens. He answered letters from students and teachers and many other people from around the world. In his spare time, he also played golf two times a week.

Shige and Ben just before Ben received
the Distinguished Service Medal in 2005

Chapter 21:

Honors and Awards

In 2002, Ben went to an Air Force get-together. Many of the people there were talking about him.

How brave he had been in the war! He had fought against both Germany and Japan. He had been the only Japanese-American gunner to fly against Japan. He had fought hard to fight for his country.

How brave and how lucky he had been to survive 58 missions! During the war, many crew members had not survived more than 10 missions!

Many of the other men there thought Ben deserved more honors. They asked the War Department to look at Ben's war records. They wanted the government to give him the Medal of Honor. That is our country's highest medal. But Ben was a humble man. He felt he did not deserve that honor. He said no.

Ben's best friend was newspaperman Cal Stewart. Cal made it his mission to remind people of Ben's story and bravery. Cal wrote letters to generals, congressmen, and even the President.

Cal wrote and printed booklets about Ben and paid for them himself. His first one was 12 pages long. He added to it. Soon it was 60 pages long. He called the booklet by one of Ben's nicknames, *Most Honorable Son*.

Those booklets told Ben's story and played a key role in Ben winning more awards. Cal sent them to people all over the country. Finally, the government agreed that Ben deserved more.

By that time, Ben had earned and received some of our country's highest honors for war service "above and beyond the call of duty." He had received three **Distinguished** Flying Crosses and an Air Medal with five oak leaf clusters. In 2005, he received another great honor, the Distinguished Service Medal.

Ben wearing his Distinguished Service Medal, 2005

Such honors and awards opened the door to four White House invitations from President George W. Bush in three years, from 2006 through 2008. One of those was a special dinner honoring the leader of Japan. That happened more than 50 years after the end of World War II!

Ben's daughter Julie Cooney, Ben, First Lady Laura Bush, Japan's Prime Minister Junichiro Koizumi, President George W. Bush, and Ben's wife Shige Kuroki at the White House in 2006
(photo by Kimberlee Hewett, courtesy of the George W. Bush Presidential Library)

On May 1, 2008, President George W. Bush told everyone about the bravery of Japanese-

Americans who served in World War II. He told

about the bravery of the 442nd Regiment. He told

about other Japanese-Americans who helped

translate Japanese war messages.

President George W. Bush and Ben Kuroki salute each other at a
special Asian American meeting at the White House in 2008
(photo by Joyce N. Boghosian, courtesy of the George W. Bush Presidential Library)

The President also told about the Army Air

Force Nisei hero—his friend Ben Kuroki. He and

Ben even saluted each other, and someone took a

picture of that salute. That was during a special

Asian American meeting at the White House. Ben

received a special **citation** or award from the President on that special day. He said it was "the most awesome moment" of his life.

That same afternoon, Ben received more honors at another program. That program was held at the Smithsonian's Air and Space Museum. The Smithsonian Museum in Washington, D.C. now has most of Ben's personal and Air Force things in its collection, so people can see them there. Ben said he was very lucky to find a home for all his "stuff" at the Smithsonian.

Ben received many national honors. He also received many honors from his home state of Nebraska. The Nebraska Press Association gave Ben its highest honor—a President's Award. The University of Nebraska gave him its highest honorary degree—a Doctor of Letters.

The University also created a Ben Kuroki Journalism **Scholarship**. That means the university now gives money each year to some students to take journalism classes. Ben always loved working with students and was always very pleased to be able to do something more for them.

Ben gave back in other ways, too. In 2010, he was invited to take part in the American Veterans Center Conference in Washington DC where he would again speak to students, **veterans**, and other people. There he received the **Audie Murphy Award**. (**Audie Murphy** was another very famous American World War II hero.) The award goes to veterans who went above and beyond the call of duty in the military and then continued to be positive role models for the rest of their lives.

Also in 2010, Ben joined with others to ask Congress to give the Nisei 442nd Regiment a Medal of Honor for their part in World War II. He was very proud of the patriotism and sacrifice of all his fellow veterans, including those who had come from the internment camps.

Ben was especially moved by the Honor Roll

that now stands at the Minidoka (Idaho) Internment Camp site. That Honor roll lists the names of those Japanese-American soldiers who were killed in action from there.

Many of them were in the 442nd Regiment of Nisei soldiers. That Minidoka Internment Camp suffered the highest number of soldiers killed in the war—65!

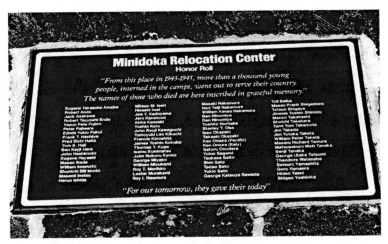

The Honor Roll at the Minidoka (Idaho) Internment Camp. This monument shows a list of 65 Japanese-American soldiers from this camp who were killed in WWII while fighting for the USA.

Ben always felt a special connection to Nisei soldiers who had lived in the internment camps.

Chapter 22:

Conclusion: Re-telling Ben's Story

Back in 2007, another Japanese American named Bill Kubota also made a special connection to Ben. He made a **documentary** to honor Ben nationally.

Bill's father, Jim Kubota, had lived in an internment camp during the war. Jim Kubota was only 13 years old when Ben came to that camp during the war. In the short time that Ben was there, he became Jim's lifelong hero.

Years later, Jim urged his own son Bill to make a documentary video about Ben's life and to call it *Most Honorable Son*, one of Ben's nicknames. The Public Broadcast System (PBS) aired Ben's story on television in September 2007, after first showing it at a special meeting in Nebraska.

Back on August 1, 2007, PBS held a special showing of Bill Kubota's program *Most Honorable Son*. It was shown at a big hotel in Lincoln, Nebraska, and was hosted by Governor Dave Heineman. Invitations were sent out to people all over the country. Tickets to the dinner and show sold for $100 a person.

More than 600 people came to meet and honor Ben Kuroki that night. Many of them were men who had flown with Ben during World War II. Others were family and friends from Hershey, including Gordy's nephew Kip Jorgenson. Still others were military and government people. The author of this book and her husband were also there—at Ben's invitation.

Ben had contacted me some months before to thank me for including him as a Nebraskan of character in my first book. That book was the *Nebraska Adventure*, an award-winning Nebraska studies textbook for 4th graders.

I then asked permission to interview Ben so we could write a children's biography book of him. And Ben invited me—and my husband—to the PBS showing, so that we could do a special five-hour interview with him the morning before that.

On the morning before the dinner show, Ben and his wife talked with us for hours. It was the beginning of a wonderful friendship. Ben and Shige talked about their family. Then Ben told the story of his life. He talked about growing up on a Nebraska farm. He talked about the war.

When Ben told about what he did in the war, his wife threw her hands high into the air. She had never heard his war stories before. She said, "I didn't know you did all that! I'm glad I didn't know you then. I wouldn't have let you go. I would have been so afraid for you!"

Then Ben told about his life after the war. He talked about his speeches to famous people. He talked about his newspaper work. He talked about meeting with President George W. Bush in the White House and meeting other famous people in wonderful places in America.

Ben also talked about how lucky he had been all his life. He showed us the tiny holes in his ears and told us his family's legend of his lucky ears. Ben and his wife had been married for many years by then, but she had never heard the story about his ears. She had never even noticed the tiny holes before! She was amazed to hear about her husband's lucky ears.

Ben's father had been right, those many years before, when he told about the legend and the tiny holes in his son's ears. Ben Kuroki was very lucky.   He lived a long life, and he did become famous.

He had many good friends who stood up for him and helped him. Ben always said, "I'm lucky to have had good friends. I was very lucky to grow up in America and Nebraska. And I'm the luckiest dude on the planet!"

But it was Ben himself who made the difference. Ben has always been a humble man. He never bragged about his own deeds or honors. He never asked for more than he deserved. He has always been an honorable man. He always tried to do the right thing. He became famous because he was very lucky, but also because of the choices he made in life.

Ben Kuroki was a hero who fought very hard for the right to fight for his country and to prove he was truly an American. He was a war hero, a patriot, and a good citizen.

Bill Kubota called him the first Japanese-

American war hero.   And President George W. Bush said, "I am proud to tell you [that] America is a better place because of you, Ben [Kuroki]." Ben Kuroki truly was a very lucky man and a true American hero.

Glossary:

442nd Regiment: an Army infantry group of Japanese-Americans who were born in the USA, and who fought for America during World War II

Air Corps or Army Air Corps: the part of the American Army that became the Air Force during World War II

canopy: a round, glass-like bubble at the top or underside of the plane where the gunner sits; sometimes called a turret

citation: a special award

citizen: someone who lives in a country legally and obeys the laws of that country

congressman: a member of congress, a politician

corps: pronounced like core, as in Army Air Corps; a group of military men with the same kind of mission, goal, or training

depression: a time in history when many people have no jobs and no money

distinguished: someone or something well-known or important

documentary: a movie or video that shows true happenings

drought: a long period of time when no rain falls and when plants and rivers dry up

Dust Bowl Days: a long, dry and dirty time in the 1930s

frostbite: a condition in which fingers, toes, or

nose freeze and turn black when exposed to extreme cold

Great Depression: 1929 through the 1930s, a very bad time for most American businesses and workers

infantry: an Army group that fights on foot

internment camp: a sort of prison camp in the USA for Japanese Americans and their immigrant parents during World War II

irrigation: water system used to grow farm crops

journalism: writing for a newspaper or magazine

legend: an old story that might or might not be true; a story handed down through a family or from one group of people to another

neutral: not taking sides. In a war, a country is neutral if it does not side with any of the countries at war.

Nisei: Japanese-Americans born in the United States but whose parents were born in Japan

patriotism: a person's strong love for his/her country and a willingness to fight for it

politician: someone involved in politics or government

racism: disliking someone just because they are of a different color, religion, culture, or background

regiment: a special group of 200 to 5,000 American Army soldiers

scholarship: a gift of money to help a student pay

for his/her college education

stock market: a place where people invest their money in other businesses to try to make a profit

turret: a clear glass-like bubble on a warplane, where the gunner sits

uniform: clothes worn by people in the Army, Air Force, Navy, police, or other kinds of services

veterans: people who have served in some branch of the military

Selected Bibliography

Fiction:
Bunting, Eve. *So Far From the Sea.* Clarion, 1998.
Patneaude, David. *Thin Wood Walls.* Sandpiper, 2008.
Mochizuki, Ken. *Baseball Saved Us.* Lee and Low, 1995.
Nonfiction:
1925-1949: The War: Nebraska Stories (Lesson Plans). http://www.nebraskastudies.org/0800/resources/09st ories.pdf
Biga, Leo Adam. "The Two Wars of Ben Kuroki," *Nebraska Life Magazine.* September/October 2007.
Cooper, Michael L. *Fighting for Honor: Japanese Americans of World War II.* Clarion, 2000.
Kral, E. A. *Profile: Ben Kuroki.* http://www.nsea.org/news/ KurokiProfile.htm
Kubota, Bill. *Most Honorable Son.* Documentary DVD and video available from PBS, 2007.
Kuroki, Ben. Interviews, phone calls, correspondence.
Lampell, Millard. "The Boy From Nebraska," *The Long Way Home* [Radio Plays]. Julian Messner, 1946.
Nebraska Trailblazers #18 Aviation in Nebraska and #21 Nebraskans in World War II. Nebraska State Historical Society. http://www.nebraskahistory.org/ museum/teachers/material/trailist.htm
Sakurai, Gail. *Japanese American Internment Camps* (Cornerstones of Freedom). Children's Press, 2007.
Sterner, C. Douglas. *Go for Broke: The Nisei Warriors of World War II Who Conquered Germany, Japan, and American Bigotry.* Clearfield, UT: American Legacy Historical Press, 2007.
Stewart, Carroll [Cal]. *The Most Honorable Son: Ben Kuroki.* Lincoln, NE: Nebraska Printing Center, various printings, 2002-2008.

Thinking Questions:
Thinking More About Ben Kuroki

1. Make a list of some positive character traits that describe Ben. Choose the one you think best describes him and tell why you chose that one. Compare with someone else's choice.

2. When Ben was born, it was not uncommon for babies to be born at home and for children to only go to school until 8th grade. Why do you think that was so?

3. What was Ben like in school? Why were his teachers and classmates surprised when Ben began speaking against racism during and after the war?

4. Ben often said that he never really felt different from other Americans when he lived in Nebraska. Why do you think that was so? Do you think it would have been the same if he had been born in another state or another time?

5. Why did people feel differently about Ben and other Japanese Americans and German Americans in the late 1930s and 1940s?

6. Why did Ben and his brother Fred want to join the Army? What made Ben fight so hard to stay in the Army Air Corps?

7. How did the other crewmen on the planes feel about Ben being Japanese American?

8. In what ways do you think Ben's childhood skills and sports helped him in the war?

9. Why were Japanese-American people put in internment camps in World War II?

10. How did the people in the internment camps feel about Ben when he came to visit?

11. How did Ben feel about being in the internment camps and about the people there?

12. Why was Ben so afraid of being in the prison camp in the desert and on the island of Tinian?

13. When Ben was finished with his first 25 missions (against Germany), he added five more. Why did he do the extra missions?

14. Why did Ben's crewmembers call him "Most Honorable Son"?

15. What was Ben's 59th mission and what did he do in this mission?

16. Why was it important for Ben to go to college after the war? How did he use his education?

17. In what ways did Ben prove that he was an American and a good citizen?

18. Why do you think Ben always called himself "the luckiest dude on the planet"?

19. After the war, Ben loved to talk to or write to teachers and students. Why do you think he did that?

20. Do you think more people need to know Ben's story? If so, why?

Index

Acknowledgements:

Ben would like to thank everyone who helped him during his many years. Unfortunately, that is not possible. For now, let us give thanks to the obvious: wife Shige, daughter Julie Cooney, sister Rosemary Ura, and all the Kuroki family; Kip and the family of Gordy Jorgenson; classmates, Deb Koch, people of Hershey, & other Nebraskans; Cal Stewart, his son Scott Stewart, Emil Reutzel, Jim Cornwell, and other newspaper people; Bill and Jim Kubota; all Ben's friends; all students and teachers who have written to Ben from around the world, including June Woodman and Sharon Bishop; Millard Lampell and Ralph Martin; airmen and crews of the 93rd Bomb Group; the Army Air Corps/Force in general; Captain James Jenkins who twice kept Ben on board his plane; Lieutenant Brannan and other military officers who listened and helped Ben serve his country; Sgt. Russell Olsen; Congressman Carl Curtis and Secretary of War Henry Stimson; three great Californians who went to bat for Ben: Dr. Monroe Deutsch, Ray Lyman Wilbur, and Chester Rowell; other members of the Commonwealth Club; Allen Beerman and the Nebraska Press Association; the Nebraska State Historical Society; the 442nd Regiment of Nisei; families from the Japanese Internment camps; all Americans who served in World War II (including my dad), other American wars (including my son), and peacetime; President George W. Bush; Jodie Steck; librarians/curators at the Smithsonian & other museums; my husband Ron Lukesh; all American citizens who love and respect their country; and everyone everywhere who has ever followed Ben's story or admired his courage, dedication, and patriotism. To all those people and many more, Ben and I humbly give thanks.

An adult biography of Ben Kuroki is also planned.

—J.A.L. (and B.K.)

LaVergne, TN USA
04 January 2011
211018LV00007B/228/P